For Perdine
love
Alan

Photograph: The New Mexico Department of Development

More than a decade ago a room at the Palace of the Governors, Museum of New Mexico, was devoted to a typical "New Mexican Ranch Room." This exhibited 19th century tools and household implements, textiles, tin pieces and *santos*, which would have been used concomitantly with the furniture pictured: a very large grain chest, a *trastero*, a *repisa*, a chair with a seat of laced rawhide thongs and—the end of which is shown—a serving table.

FURNITURE OF SPANISH NEW MEXICO

Alan C. Vedder

Photography by David Donoho

The Sunstone Press

Santa Fe, New Mexico

FIRST EDITION

Book Design — Douglas J. Houston

Printed in the United States of America

Library of Congress Cataloging in Publication Data

Vedder, Alan C.   1912 -
    Furniture of Spanish New Mexico.

    1. Furniture, Spanish American — New Mexico.
 2. Furniture, Colonial — New Mexico. I. Title.
NK2435.N6V43   749.2'189   76-50322
ISBN 0 - 913270 - 67 - 9
ISBN 0 - 913270 - 66 - 0 pbk.

Published in 1977 by The Sunstone Press.
Post Office Box 2321, Santa Fe, New Mexico 87501

To Ann

Whose great interest in and feeling for the Spanish culture
has helped in every phase of this book

Acknowledgements

My first and deepest gratitude is to the late E. Boyd, through whose knowledge, guidance and friendship I learned about the culture of Spanish New Mexico. We shared the same office and conservation laboratory for 20 years. We discussed thoroughly each object which came to our attention as a possible addition to the Spanish Colonial collections at the Museum of New Mexico. Without the wisdom and personal experience that E. Boyd imparted, including practical observations and actual conservation work on many pieces of furniture, this book could not have been written.

I am also especially grateful to the many private collectors in New Mexico, who asked to be anonymous, but who permitted their households to be upset in order to photograph their furniture, most of the pieces for the first time. A special effort was made to include in this book examples of furniture not heretofore photographed or described, in order to broaden the scope of what is in print and thus have a wider basis for establishing New Mexican styles.

Many persons in museums and other organizations were of great assistance, and I am deeply grateful to the staff and their institutions: the American Museum in Britain, Bath, England; the Millicent A. Rogers Memorial Museum, Taos, New Mexico; the Museum of Albuquerque, Albuquerque, New Mexico; the State Records Center & Archives and the Museum of New Mexico, Santa Fe, New Mexico.

The cheerful cooperation of the photographer, David Donoho, is much appreciated, and I am also grateful to Laura Gilpin for permitting her photographs to be used. I acknowledge with gratitude the assistance and encouragement of friends and of my wife, who ably handled editing and details of this book.

Alan C. Vedder
Santa Fe, New Mexico

Table of Contents

Introduction

Traditional Spanish New Mexican furniture can best be characterized as simple, having straight lines and good, honest proportions, all of which give these pieces a particular type of dignity. As is true of other handmade objects in a given society, furniture made in New Mexico mirrored the lives of New Mexicans in the 18th and 19th centuries— isolation and a rugged existence. The earliest furniture was made for churches and a few rich families. Even well into the 19th century, the average home was devoid of pieces considered common today: chairs, tables and beds.

The author regards the traditional period in Spanish New Mexican furniture to begin about 1776 and extend until almost 1900. Those pieces that survive illustrate the important contributions made by the Spanish in the 18th and 19th centuries to this form of the decorative arts. Except for construction fragments, nothing is left in New Mexico dating prior to the Reconquest in 1693. Moreover, nothing remains from the early part of the 18th century, no doubt due to constant reusing and reworking of every piece of furniture until it was literally worn out, as was the case with the tools used. Despite outside influences in the 19th century, furniture made in New Mexico continued to exhibit definite traditional New Mexican elements until close to the beginning of the 20th century and even somewhat later in isolated mountain areas. Such furniture could still be made today by a sensitive person using old-style tools. Several years ago a Spanish American carpenter, who was a friend of the author, did exactly that. He chopped down a tree in the mountains and worked the wood using only old-style tools to make a chest in the traditional manner. After some aging of the wood to attain a proper patina, the chest resembled in every way the old ones made a century or more ago in New Mexico.

One factor that merits serious consideration is the conservatism of the Spanish people. This, perhaps as much as anything else, resulted in the making of furniture over a 125-year period which, while it showed evolution and change, still retained certain characteristics producing a definite, recognizable New Mexican style. A main purpose of this book, through its descriptions and photographs of styles and construction, is to help individuals recognize traditional New Mexican furniture, whether the piece is found in Santa Fe, in New England or in California.

Outside influences had a long way to travel: up through Mexico over the Chihuahua Trail, where a one-way caravan journey took six months, and later over the Santa Fe Trail from the Missouri River towns. Compare this with European migration directly to the eastern United States. Furthermore, the Spanish were sometimes almost a century behind other Europeans in various art fields. This situation was emphasized in the colonies by the laws of the Spanish Crown, which carefully monopolized trade, thus precluding outside influences and perpetuating Spanish traditions in all lines, including arts and crafts.

While the census of 1790 listed 14 carpenters in Santa Fe and nine in Albuquerque, probably only a part of their work involved furniture. It is reasonable to expect that most New Mexicans had to be self-sufficient, making a few simple pieces of furniture for their own homes. The following is indicative of the fact that many homes were sparsely furnished even into the 20th century. About two decades ago an older person of modest means in Santa Fe was asked about the use of a little stool or *taramita*. The reply was "no, it was not used for traveling, it was used in our home; we either sat on that or on the floor."

While the makers of most New Mexican furniture remain anonymous, the author believes that *santeros*, having skills at working with wood, probably also made furniture. A cartographer from near Burgos, Spain, Captain Bernardo Miera y Pacheco, arrived in New Mexico in 1756 and died there in 1785. He also made *santos*; one of his *retablos* at the Museum of New Mexico, inscribed with a date of 1780, is in its original heavily grooved frame. Being an ambitious man with many interests, having once even asked permission to cast a cannon, it is unlikely that someone else made the frame for him or that it was imported into New Mexico. This deep grooving is virtually identical to that on the stiles and rails of many 18th century pieces of furniture. Another dated carpentry piece with similar heavy grooving is the double doors at *El Santuario de Chimayo*, dated 1816. Some furniture examples during the first half of the 19th century can be attributed by style and brushwork to the *santeros* Molleno, the "Santo Nino" *santero* and Rafael Aragon; these are illustrated in this book.

In New Mexican furniture the wood almost always used was Ponderosa pine, as it was the only type of large workable wood locally available. The furniture illustrated in this book is made of pine unless otherwise noted. In the absence of sawmills until 1847, when the first one was built in Santa Fe, wood was hand adzed and also planed on the outer surfaces for a smoother finish. As furniture was entirely handmade, no two pieces were alike. The boards were put together in a variety of ways, the most common being mortise and tenon. In almost all cases in New Mexico during the traditional period the tenon passed entirely through the board in which the mortise was cut, creating a so-called through or exposed tenon. This type of construction can be seen in most of the furniture illustrated here. Another New Mexican mortise and tenon characteristic was the insertion of wedges of wood into the tenon to make the joint tighter. Other construction methods used included doweling, often with square dowels, and dovetailing, which was most often seen on the corner of chests, although it was sometimes covered up with applied moldings. Beginning about 1825, when new hand tools arrived, it became possible to make tongue and groove edges, and this was frequently done with boards making up the tops of tables and chests and, in the case of one chest pictured here, almost the entire box was constructed with tongue and groove boards. The new tools also permitted a refinement of dovetailing, so that the wedges were more uniform and closer to the shape of doves' tails rather than being more or less rectangular as they had been in the 18th century. Due to the scarcity of iron, New Mexican hardware was extremely simple, as for example eyelet hinges, which were also used in Spain. Also because of this metal scarcity, nails were not used in original construction until well into the 19th century. Even then most New Mexican pieces continued to be mortised and tenoned, a process which was stronger and more permanent than nailing. Nails have, however, been used to strengthen and repair many old pieces.

New Mexican 18th century furniture followed closely the Spanish traditions of the 16th and 17th centuries. Tools were then supplied by the Crown and declined in supply in the early 19th century. Traditional Spanish motifs of pomegranates, rosettes, shells, lions and scallops were carved in deep relief done by gouging. Other decorative techniques employed were heavy grooving and cutouts on the bottom of rails, often in "S" curves, such as had been done on 17th century furniture in Spain. Hand-carved spindles and splats were used. The spindles were a logical adaptation of the *Mudejar* grilles in Spain. The use of multiple splats on chairs and benches appears to be a peculiarity to New Mexico and other Spanish areas. Although used earlier on architectural details, it was not until near the end of the 18th century that New Mexican furniture was decorated with pleasing chip carved designs, a *Mudejar* influence direct from Spain.

After the first quarter of the 19th century some changes took place in New Mexican furniture. Traders from the east arrived not only with new hand tools, but also with new ideas that gradually modified the design and decoration of furniture. Influences of the Directory and Empire styles, which were adapted in making chairs and daybeds, probably came from both the east over the Santa Fe Trail and the south from Mexico over the Chihuahua Trail. In an official document of 1831 listing persons who arrived in New Mexico over the Santa Fe Trail to become naturalized citizens, five carpenters from diverse areas are listed: two from St. Louis, one from New York, one from Great Britain and one from France. Any one of these could have brought in the new styles. On the other hand, Chihuahua was a center for the Empire style in the 19th century. Not only have many of these pieces come to Santa Fe in recent years, but also the area is still filled with numerous examples of the Empire style.

Designs carved in geometric shapes and those utilizing applied wood pieces became popular by the mid-19th century, as did the use of decorations incised with a compass. Later, applied designs became more elaborate, often in the Victorian style. Relief carving became shallower and was done only on each design itself, rather than by gouging the entire background. Many of the 18th century design elements continued to be used, however, as did the traditional construction methods previously discussed. New Mexico was still largely isolated during the 19th century, and its people continued to adhere to their established traditions. Only toward the close of the century did most New Mexican furniture begin to show a considerable amount of outside influence. A most unusual case is a late 19th century chair made after the style of Charles Locke Eastlake, an English furniture designer of that period. As this is considered an exception, no photograph of it was included in this book.

Much of the furniture made in New Mexico today, as well as earlier in the 20th century, utilizes elaborate decorative embellishments, a poor sense of proportion and other construction elements which produce objects distinctly heavy in feeling. They often look more like copies of poorly made Mexican pieces. It is the author's hope that this book with its photographs and descriptions of authentic pieces, as well as the tools used by the craftsmen, will encourage the revitalization of traditional designs in order to make simple furniture of good proportions with a restraint of decoration, which will fit extremely well into today's New Mexican homes. This simple furniture has the added advantage of mixing well with good furniture of other American and European periods.

Within each category of furniture in this book the pieces are arranged chronologically so that the developments and persistent traditions discussed above can be observed. While the author regards the dating of New Mexican furniture by style and construction to be reasonably accurate in most cases, it is hoped that in the near future some pieces can be checked by dendrochronology (tree-ring dating of wood). When this method was used in the past for some *santos*, the dates turned out to be practically identical to those arrived at by a consideration of styles.

About Conservation —

Spanish Colonial furniture can be restored and because of its scarcity should be, if one has the main parts, such as the frame of a table or the seat, stiles and a slat or two of a chair. The principal point to remember is that work must be done by hand, never with power tools. A perfectly cut mortise and tenon creates an artificiality that is easily recognizable. Securing of loose pieces should be done with hand-whittled dowels and sometimes glue, such as *Elmer's*. At the same time any nails which have been added should be removed.

If a newly acquired piece is received in sound condition, the only conservation usually necessary is to vacuum the boards, clean them with turpentine and then wax all surfaces (including the underside and any drawer interiors) with a clear paste wax, such as clear *Trewax*, which contains carnauba, the hardest of waxes. Polishing with a brush produces a soft satiny finish, which will, of course, dull in time. Some private owners prefer to give their pieces repeated waxings to maintain the sheen, but this is not typical of New Mexican furniture.

The best preserved furniture is rather light in color, as was the pine originally, although dirt and age have darkened some pieces. The Spanish in New Mexico did not stain the wood but left the color alone. However, in addition to decoratively painted and sometimes gessoed pieces, a few were originally colored with paints. On the other hand, heavier oil paint is invariably a later addition, the removal of which is an individual aesthetic decision. If it is decided to remove this later painting, the patina is usually enriched by leaving some paint on the surfaces, rather than removing it entirely. In any case, the piece should be waxed.

Some attractive examples, particularly chairs, are old assemblages of parts from different pieces. These should not be discarded. Not only are they usually pleasing in appearance, but they illustrate an important aspect of the history of New Mexican furniture—that of reworking old pieces.

During his investigations for specific furniture to be illustrated in this book, the author was saddened to learn that many families who once owned these pieces no longer did. Many had been broken up for firewood, taken to the dump or otherwise discarded in favor of modern furniture. Hopefully, appreciation of the surviving old pieces will increase, and even those in deteriorated condition will be saved and restored.

FURNITURE OF
SPANISH NEW MEXICO

Alan C. Vedder

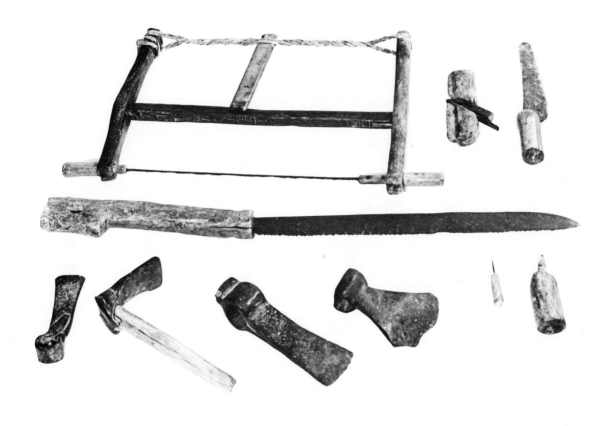

Left to right: *Top — bucksaw; plane; knife*
                    Middle — single hafted saw (34¾" long, blade 21")
                    Bottom — adz; adz with handle; ax; ax; awl; knife

*Owners: The Museum of New Mexico, the Historical Society of New Mexico and the Spanish
        Colonial Arts Society, Inc.*

The tools available to New Mexicans in the 18th and early 19th centuries were of the same types as had been used in Spain for centuries. For example, a type of bucksaw, which is pictured here, was depicted in a Spanish Romanesque fresco done in 1100 and also in Peruvian Colonial art. This particular saw was purchased in Spain where it was still being used in 1961. It is the only one in the photograph of the types of tools used in the 18th and 19th centuries not from New Mexico; although there is an identical one in Santa Fe, it was not available to be photographed. The only other principal tools used, examples of which the author was unable to locate, are the chisel and augur.

These tools had their specific limitations, a factor which produced simple furniture of a definite, identifiable style. They were reused and resharpened until completely worn out. The listing of tools in wills of this period indicates their value and scarcity.

After the opening of the Santa Fe Trail in 1821, traders brought in a variety of new and improved hand tools including planes, which were more versatile than the Spanish ones, and much sturdier saws.

18

Photographer: Laura Gilpin

Although sparse in furniture, this 18th century room, as exhibited in the Museum of International Folk Art, Museum of New Mexico in 1959, illustrates the dearth of domestic furniture available during that period. Various tools, horse trappings, domestic implements, a few *santos*, wooden sconces and shutters adorn the room, together with blankets hanging from a pole, below which can be seen the edge of a folded homemade mattress stuffed with wool. The rawhide chest is from Mexico—many of these were brought here—and the New Mexican pieces include an *alacena*, a *repisa*, a carved chest and *taramitas*. Rooms such as this one existed in New Mexico 200 years ago—at the time of the signing of the Declaration of Independence.

Photographer: Laura Gilpin

Compared with the 18th century room exhibited at the Museum of International Folk Art at the same time as this one in 1959, this 19th century room looks impressive. *Santos*, colcha embroidery and an attractive mantelpiece give warmth to this room. Edges of a day-bed and a *repisa* are visible on the left. A handsome *santero* painted *trastero* in the corner dominates the room (see page 47 for its description), next to which is a painted chest, similar to the two illustrated in this book on pages 32 and 33. On the right side is a straight chair, a simple table and a chair in the Directory style.

Chests

Chests are the earliest type of furniture made. Because of this, and their wide variety of storage purposes, they comprise the largest category in this book. They were necessary for the secure storage of possessions and were used for both church and domestic purposes. The latter included the storing of valuables, household articles and clothing, as well as grain, dried fruit and other food items, which were vital to New Mexicans for survival through the winter. The diverse chests pictured here illustrate not only the various uses, but also the typical changes in construction and design over a 125-year period. Note that chests with legs were not made in New Mexico before the end of the 18th century.

All furniture in this section is made of pine.

Measurements: H. 24½", W. 46¾", D. 22½"
Date: Circa 1775
Owner: The Spanish Colonial Arts Society, Inc., on loan to the Museum of New Mexico
Accession Number: L.5.75-69

Probably the earliest piece of furniture illustrated in this book, this chest was undoubtedly carved by Nicolas de Apodaca, who did considerable woodwork in the church at Las Trampas when it was being built in the 1770's. The author is also exploring the possibility that Nicolas de Apodaca could have been an 18th century *santero*. The front of this chest is heavily carved with the traditional Spanish motifs of a large 23-petaled rosette and pomegranates near the upper corners. The design of branches used on this chest and on the pulpit at Las Trampas no doubt came from the stone altar screen completed in Santa Fe in 1761 by stone carvers from Mexico; this altar screen is now in *Cristo Rey* Church. The ends of this chest are not carved but only painted in red and green oils, as is the front of the chest; the rosette on one end has ten petals and on the other eight. The top and back are plain. The hasp and hinges are old replacements, while the escutcheon is probably original. As the photograph shows, the ends are dovetailed to the back and front, and the bottom is doweled to the box.

The close-up shows the 18th century style of carving—removing the background by gouging so that the design elements stand in deep relief. It also shows the wearing away of old paint.

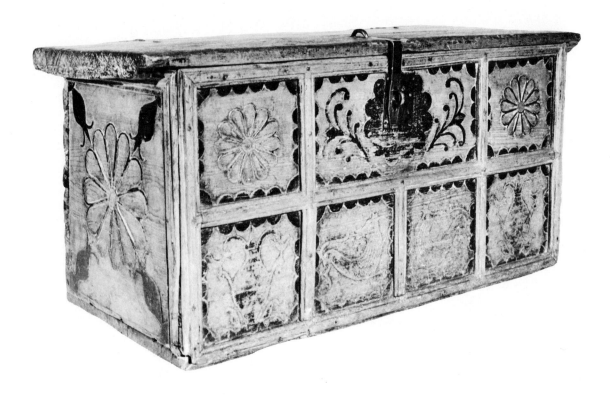

Measurements: H. 20½", W. 43½" (lid), D. 19"
Date: 18th century, last quarter
Owner: The Museum of New Mexico
Accession Number: A.60.20-1

The carving of this traditional 18th century chest was done by gouging out the background so that the remaining wood stood in relief in the designs as shown. To emphasize the designs, the parts which were not carved were painted a brown-black. Notice the scallops around the seven front panels, the branches around the escutcheon and the pomegranates at the ends. Other brown-black painting makes the rosettes, lions and pomegranates stand out even more. Grooved molding separates the panels and also conceal, for a finer finish, dovetailing at the corners. The hardware is not original but old, handmade, suitable replacements. The interior has two tiers of six square drawers each, below which is a single larger drawer. This was said to be a *cajon de las donas* or a woman's storage chest.

Measurements: H. 25'', W. 48¾'', D. 23¾''
Date: Circa 1800
Owner: The School of American Research, on loan to the Museum of New Mexico
Photographer: Laura Gilpin

This appealing chest incorporates on its front the carving of four rampant lions, two rabbits, a small rosette, two branches, three pomegranates and scallops on all four edges. The patch, which can be seen on the upper right of the scalloping is probably original and done to cover up a knot hole. On the left end of the chest is a crowned lion and a pheasant-like bird; on the right is only a crowned lion. The iron work is old. Notice the dovetailing at the ends. The chest sits on an old stand, made of two separate parts, each of which is made of three pieces of wood, mortised and tenoned.

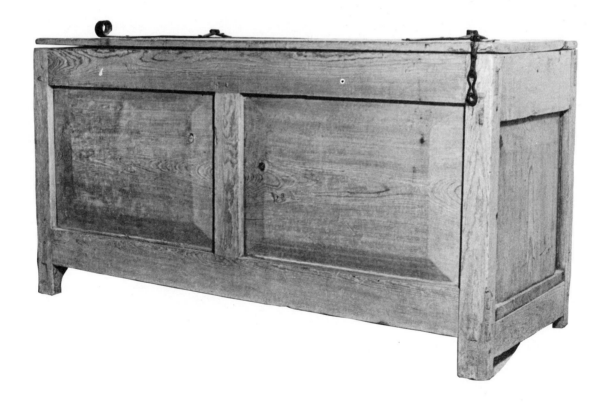

Measurements: H. 35½″, W. 70¾″, D. 26″
Date: Circa 1800
Owner: Private Collection

This handsome large chest in remarkably good condition has two simple large panels on the front beveled on all four sides. On the ends the single panel is beveled only at the top and sides. The iron work is original and unusual as the hinges extend from the back to the front ending in a loop, one of which is missing, and the hasp is at the right corner instead of being in the middle. The wood of this chest, which is hand adzed and planed, has a stunning patina.

At least seven chests of this general design exist, each with diagonal braces and chip carving. However, each one varies in design and measurements. The boards are adzed, with outer sides smoothed with a plane, which is typical of Spanish Colonial furniture of New Mexico. The two front panels are gouged out with a chisel in a rectangular design with a circle in the center of each and chip carving around each panel, on the rails, stiles and upright piece in the center and the diagonals. Each end has a beveled panel with some chip carving around it and on the applied piece at the bottom.

Measurements: H. 31", W. 34¼", D. 15¾"
Date: 19th century, first part
Owner: The Spanish Colonial Arts Society, Inc., on loan to the Museum of New Mexico
Accession Number: L.5.75-78

This example is in excellent condition except for two burned spots on the lid. The overhang pieces of the lid are dovetailed to it. The iron work is original, including the key.

Measurements: H. 30", W. 53", D. 18¾"
Date: 19th century, first part
Owner: The Millicent A. Rogers Memorial Museum, Taos, New Mexico

This chest is more rectangular in design than the preceding one, with longer diagonals attached near the bottom of the legs. The escutcheon is original, while the hasp and hinges are missing. The overhang pieces of the lid have been sawed off; on one end two tenons or tongues are left.

Measurements: H. 42", W. 30¾", D. 18"
Date: Circa 1825
Owner: Wadsworth Atheneum, Hartford, Connecticut
Accession Number: 1926.301
Photographer: E. Irving Blomstrann

The construction and decorative elements of this chest can perhaps illustrate the beginning of the influence on New Mexican furniture work of the small tools which came over the Santa Fe Trail after its opening in 1821. These were superior to those available at that time from Mexico, and they created a departure from previous strict adherence to 17th and 18th century Spanish designs. Straight outlines and circles on this chest were incised with a primitive compass. The tongue and groove construction of the two boards on the lid, the front one of which opens, indicates the arrival of new tools. The overall composition of the designs, including the undulating ribbon motif, are in pleasing proportions. This chest is probably an outgrowth of the previous two illustrated chip carved, diagonally-braced ones, with similar design elements apparent.

Measurements: H. 29½", W. 66½", D. 18"
Date: 1804-45
Owner: The Museum of New Mexico
Accession Number: A.59.11-1

This gessoed and painted chest was originally in the church at Ranchos de Taos. Its brush strokes and colors indicate that it was undoubtedly painted by Molleno, a *santero* whose working dates were 1804-45. The front and ends are carved in relief in geometric designs, then gessoed and painted in black, red, blue and yellow watercolors. The interior has a compartment at one end for small items. This is the right type of chest for vestment and sacristy storage.

Measurements: H. 24½", W. 33½", D. 15"
Date: 1804-45
Owner: The American Museum in Britain, Bath, England
Accession Number: 61.266
Photographer: Derek Balmer

This piece, as the preceding one, is attributed to the *santero* Molleno. When the author collected this small chest for the permanent exhibit of New Mexican rooms at the American Museum in Britain, it was covered with green oil paint, which was removed. This revealed traces of Molleno's gesso and paint on the front with a clearer design of flowers at the ends. The stiles and two horizontals are grooved, while the overhangs of the lid are dovetailed to it. The use of six boards applied to the front, to create five sections, is similar to the decoration of the two following chests.

Measurements: H. 27¾", W. 46½", D. 21"
Date: 19th century, second quarter
Owner: Private Collection

This chest is painted red with the applied boards, which are planed and grooved, painted black, making a handsome combination. The lid has overhangs at the ends which are dovetailed to it. The hardware is original, although part of the hasp is lost.

Measurements: H. 24¼", W. 26", D. 21½"
Date: 19th century, second quarter
Owner: Private Collection

Panels on the front and ends of this chest are made by grooved applied pieces, which are doweled to the frame. Additional designs are created by grooving of the stiles, by chip carving of the lowest applied horizontals and by grooving, chip carving and cutout work (mostly worn away) on the front and side skirts. The entire top, which is without hinges, lifts off. Inside there is a single compartment at one end raised off the bottom. The chest was undoubtedly used for domestic articles.

Measurements: H. 17¼", W. 35", D. 15"
Date: 19th century, second quarter
Owner: Taylor Museum, Colorado Springs Fine Arts Center, Colorado Springs, Colorado
Accession Number: TM 1417
Photographer: W. L. Bowers

Further proof that *santeros* gessoed and painted objects in addition to *santos* was discovered at the Taylor Museum, when the author was there as a consultant in May 1976. This gessoed and water-colored chest is the work of the "Santo Nino" *santero*, who made both *retablos* and *bultos*. In addition, a small wooden *nicho* made by him was discovered at the same time at the Taylor Museum. As on his *santos*, this *santero* painted the chest with simple, clean-cut lines in pure colors, and he utilized repeated designs similar to those on the *nicho* and his *santos*. Notice the two birds on the front of this handsome piece.

These chests painted with oils, often with amusing scenes uncommon to New Mexico, remind one of chests from Mexico. In fact this was thought to be the case until the wood was analyzed and proven to be upper Rio Grande pine. It became apparent that a Mexican painter traveled north with his oil paints and decorated dozens of these many-colored trousseau chests with scenes and designs familiar to him. One chest by this same maker, not herein illustrated, shows a crude rendition of eleven fishermen wearing top hats in a crescent moon shaped boat.

Measurements: H. 16″, W. 29½″, D. 15″
Date: Circa 1830
Owner: Private Collection

This scene is of two men standing surrounded by a typical border of flowers. There is a sign in the center, which is indistinct. The dark indigo blue background on the front is over-painted in pink, yellow, white and a deep reddish orange. This latter color is the background for the ends, which are also painted with a typical design of three wavy lines with leaf-like motifs beside them from a central point in the ends. Touches of paint remain on the lid. The hardware is original.

Measurements: H. 14¼", W. 29", D. 13¾"
Date: Circa 1830
Owner: Private Collection

The front of this chest portrays a simple scene of two dogs and a large vase in the center surrounded by flowers. The outer border is painted red, inside of which are comma-like designs in light blue. A single white rose is painted on each end. The background is black, and the designs are white and various shades of pink and green.

Measurements: H. 30½", W. 29¾", D. 18½"
Date: 19th century, first half
Owner: The Spanish Colonial Arts Society, Inc., on loan to the Museum of New Mexico
Accession Number: L.5.75-8

What is unusual about this chest is its carving on all four sides—the only one discovered thus far to have carving, and not just paneling, on the back. The center on all four sides is carved in simple relief. The skirts both front and back, but not on the sides, are carved on the bottom in "V" shapes and scallops. The lid is plain and of a single slab. The hardware is not original, but of the traditional style.

Measurements: H. 37", W. 51", D. 19¾"
Date: Pre-1846
Owner: The Spanish Colonial Arts Society, Inc., on loan to the Museum of New Mexico
Accession Number: L.5.55-27
Photographer: Laura Gilpin

The distinctive features of this chest are the four vertical lozenge-shaped relief designs on the front, which are repeated as a single horizontal one on each end. All rails and vertical pieces including stiles are grooved and beaded with a plane, as are the lozenge reliefs on the front. The back, ends and lid are each made from a single slab. The wrought iron strap hinges are inlaid inside the lid, and the hasp and round, scalloped iron escutcheon of old New Mexican style may have been a later addition.

Measurements: H. 25½", W. 28½", D. 15½"
Date: Circa 1845
Owner: The Museum of New Mexico
Accession Number: A.71.31-196

Straw appliqued chests of this size are rare; only three are known at this time, one of which has a flat lid. This one has a replaced hutch top with newly made, but old-style, hardware. The top and bottom rails are scalloped on the inside, and the stiles are chip carved on the inner edges. The legs, which are extensions of the stiles, are chamfered, more deeply near the middle, and the carving at the bottom creates decorative feet. Charcoal black paint sets off flower decorations of appliqued cornhusk on the front and ends.

Measurements: H. 22¼", W. 26½", D. 15"
Date: 1850
Owner: Private Collection

This beautiful hutch top chest of moderate size is enhanced by attractive yellow paint partially worn off so that the grain of the wood shows in many places. A chest such as this one would have been used for domestic storage purposes. The central panel on the front, which is framed by grooved moldings, is decorated with scalloped pieces added to the top and bottom. The ends are similarly treated with smaller decorations in scale to their size. The bottom of the skirt is carved in simple rising curves like the scallops. The small curved arch at the bottom of the legs complements the decorations on the box and skirt.

Measurements: H. 34½'', W. 54'', D. 24¾''
Date: 19th century
Owner: Private Collection

This simple-appearing grain chest with its large boards has much character. It is impossible to say exactly when during the 19th century it was made. It is obviously a country piece and is said to have come from La Jolla, Socorro County, New Mexico. The long and wide central front board and the two vertical boards at each end are beveled. These are all fitted, in a tongue and groove type of construction, into the rails and stiles. The top is three boards. The lid opening is formed by a larger board at the front and a smaller one behind, tongue and grooved. These are attached to a smaller back board by hand forged hinges made by a blacksmith on Canyon Road in Santa Fe in the traditonal style. The escutcheon is original, as is probably the hasp. At one time the chest was painted red; some color remains adding patina and richness to the piece.

Measurements: H. 36¾'', W. 63½'', D. 30''
Date: Middle 19th century
Owner: Private Collection, on loan to the Museum of Albuquerque

The angular slants of the uprights on the top front of this grain chest create an unusual design pattern. This is emphasized by the carved half circles, in varying sizes, the shapes of which are created by a compass. The moderately grooved stiles and horizontals add further decoration. The top of the chest has applied gallery moldings except where the opening is. Being part of a room exhibit at a museum, ears of corn and a large wooden scoop of pinto beans are displayed on the top. The bright colored calico cloth attached to the wall was a common practice in 19th century New Mexican households to keep the calcimine on the wall off clothing.

Measurements: H. 39¼", W. 71", D. 32"
Date: Middle 19th century
Owner: Private Collection

This chest for grain storage has carved geometric designs on two front panels, similar to those on the *trastero* on page 50. The other four panels in the front are plain with wide applied moldings around them. Two vertical panels at each end have similar molding treatment. For access to storage there is a hinged opening in the front center of the top 37 inches wide by 18½ inches deep; the hasp is original. The top has an applied gallery except for the front of the opening. Rails and stiles are molded with a plane. The mortise and tenon construction is visible. Five boards have been added to the bottom to raise the chest off the floor.

Measurements: H. 31½″, W. 72″, D. 22¾″
Date: Middle of the 19th century
Owner: Private Collection

A most unusual feature of this hutch top grain chest is that the top is virtually perfectly shaped to hold saddles. It is the only one of its kind that the author has seen. The front, back and ends are each one piece of thick wood (1½ inches) dovetailed, and the three horizontal hutch boards are dovetailed to the ends of the lid. There are also hand forged nails in the piece. This chest is entirely original, including the three long hinges that extend over the hutch top, with the hasp attached to the end of the center one.

Measurements: H. 18¼", W. 44", D. 17½"
Date: 19th century, last half
Owner: Wadsworth Atheneum, Hartford, Connecticut
Accession Number: 1950.831
Photographer: E. Irving Blomstrann

One of the main interests of this chest is that it has been added to at a later date, a practice not uncommon with New Mexican pieces. The four rosettes are original; however, the hand scratched lions, that look like dogs, and scallops are probably early 20th century additions, possibly done by an artist to make the piece look more Spanish or by a dealer to make it more attractive to customers. The escutcheon is too fancy for this chest and for the period, but the hasp and hinges could be original.

Measurements: Chest — H. 21", W. 38¼", D. 22"; Stand — 16½" H.
Date: Circa 1880
Owner: Private Collection

The elaborate cutout appliqued to the front of the chest and carved in a fairly matching fashion on the front of its original stand make this piece outstanding. This country-made furniture, probably from the mountains, is painted green including the top, with the appliqued pieces painted blue, a colorful combination. The bold cutouts are each one piece of wood. The designs at each end are a single appliqued square of wood surrounded by appliqued moldings. Applied pieces of wood create the overhang of the lid. Square nails are used in construction. The small lock and hinges are original.

Trasteros

Trasteros are often regarded as being the most "New Mexican" of all furniture made there. Their designs can be traced directly to Spain; the Museum of New Mexico has two from that country, which are very similar to those made locally. These cupboards are popular pieces in private houses, where they fit in well because of their narrow depth and because they have shelves useful for storage of dishes, books, etc. The *trasteros* pictured here are representative of the many styles made. After the introduction of eastern-made kitchen meat safes late in the 19th century, fewer *trasteros* were made in New Mexico.

All furniture in this section is made of pine.

Measurements: H. 89″, W. 37″, D. 18¼″
Date: 18th century, last quarter
Owner: Private Collection

A distinctive feature of this handsome *trastero* is that it is painted with designs on the front and sides, possibly the work of a *santero*. It also combines various unusual interior elements, occasionally found individually in other surviving *trasteros*: tiers of drawers with hidden or secret storage behind; scooped out round depressions about three inches in diameter on the bottom shelf, the purpose of which is presently unknown, possibly to hold containers or small objects with rounded bottoms or tokens; original front edging of shelves in the top half. Another interesting feature is the presence of the two original keys; the hardware is all original. The front crest is a replacement, while the side crests are original. Construction is mortise and tenon. There is grooving on the stiles, horizontal boards and uprights of the doors.

Measurements: H. 80", W. 36", D. 12"
Date: 18th century, last quarter
Owner: The Fred Harvey Foundation, on loan to the Museum of New Mexico
Accession Number: L.69.23-63

Touches of red and green paint remain on this *trastero*. It is hand adzed and planed, mortised and tenoned with wedges, doweled and pegged. Its legs have been cut off, and the center scallop shell on the front crest is lost. The top part has three shelves, the upper two of which have an edging carved in scallops. Two of the drawers in the bottom part are missing. Eyelet hinges and locks on both the top and bottom are original. Note the well-grooved panels on the bottom doors; this same treatment is applied to the ends of the *trastero*, which are divided into two panels. Also the door frames and horizontal boards are heavily grooved.

Measurements: H. 64", W. 23¾", D. 13"
Date: Early 19th century
Owner: The Historical Society of New Mexico, Museum of New Mexico
Accession Number: BFO 83/2-8

This *trastero* is one of the simplest but most attractive made in New Mexico. It has a single puncheon door with twelve hand-carved spindles and a panel below. At one time it was painted red. The front crest is missing, but the two side ones remain, both with "V" cutouts at the top. Each end has one large panel. The two top shelves have an edging carved in scallops for decoration and perhaps to keep articles from sliding off when the door was opened. Notice how high (15¾ inches) the storage part is off the floor, a protection against rodents.

Measurements: H. 88" including shell, W. 33½", D. 12¾"
Date: 19th century, second quarter
Ownership: The School of American Research, on loan to the Museum of New Mexico
Accession Number: A.7.49-27
Photographer: Laura Gilpin

Notice the bold designs painted on the interior of the doors of this *trastero*. The swirling rose-like designs in red, indigo blue and black resemble the work of the *santero* Rafael Aragon, whose working dates coincide with the age of this piece. The back and sides of the interior also were once decorated, but the painting is now washed off. The shelves are original, as are the hardware and key. Panels of the exterior of the doors, which have four-petaled rosettes carved in the center, are painted to look like marble. This is a later addition over probably *santero* painting similar to the inside. The large front crest shell, which is original, is painted pumpkin color at the bottom and yellow and green on the carved ribs, topped by yellow scallops with green dots; black wavy lines decorate the entire shell. Notice the cutout designs on the bottom of the skirt.

Measurements: H. 62" to top of front crest, W. 33", D. 14½"
Date: 19th century, first half
Owner: Private Collection

This *trastero* illustrates the simple, clean-cut designs of traditional Spanish New Mexican furniture. The front crest is original except for a small area on the upper left corner. One side crest is original; the other is a replacement. To raise the *trastero* off the floor, about four and one-half inches were added to the legs, which had been cut down or worn. Often the back legs of *trasteros* were cut so that they would stand straight as dirt floors would be higher next to the wall due to wear in the center of the room. This piece of furniture was in a house in Abiquiu, New Mexico, at least as early as the first decade of the 20th century.

Measurements: H. 68", W. 32¾", D. 14½"
Date: Prior to 1846
Owner: The Spanish Colonial Arts Society, Inc., on loan to the Museum of New Mexico
Accession Number: L.5.55-26

This *trastero* has a simple adaptation of "linen fold" carving on the six panels of the doors. The edges of the "linen fold" designs are triple grooved, as are the uprights and cross members of the doors and a single panel at each end. The front crest is missing, but the two pieces of wood with "S" curve designs, which slip into grooves and form end crests, are original. Eyelet hinges are original; the escutcheon is a replacement. Originally there were four shelves, but now one is missing. On the left side of the bottom shelf are six scooped out round depressions two to three inches in diameter, like those in the *trastero* on page 44.

Measurements: 73½" to top of crest, W. 34¼", D. 16"
Date: Middle 19th century
Owner: Private Collection

The outstanding feature of this *trastero* is its carved geometric designs. Compare this with the chest on page 39. Each of the six panels of the door, which are attached with replaced iron hinges, have carved designs made up of four triangles with a diamond in the center. (There is a burned spot on the upper right door.) There are three panels on each side. The front crest is original, as is one side crest.

Measurements: H. 54" to top of finials, W. 33½", D. 13"
Date: 19th century, last half
Owner: Private Collection

This *trastero*, which was once painted dark red, has two puncheon doors with elaborate hand-carved spindle treatment. The ends also have spindles. The stiles end in finials on all four corners. The three shelves are beveled at the front, and each shelf is cut out at the ends to fit between the end spindles. Although the frames of the doors are replacements, all of the spindles are original. This *trastero* is one of the most complete of its type that the author has seen.

Measurements: H. 57½", W. 32½", D. 20½"
Date: Late 19th century
Owner: The Spanish Colonial Arts Society, Inc., on loan to the Museum of New Mexico
Accession Number: L.5.58-11
Photographer: Laura Gilpin

The chair in the photograph is described on the top of page 80.

This curiously squat, deep shape suggests a kitchen cupboard rather than the 18th century tall secretary-style of *trastero* which was used for documents, money, jewelry and other valuables. It was probably country-made, copying eastern meat safe cupboards with punched tin panels, by someone who had no tin and ingeniously contrived the perforations in the favorite cruciform pattern of his day. These perforations on the top panels of the doors and ends provide air circulation and incidentally add decoration. Old green house paint is almost worn off.

Alacenas

A practical device for storage in adobe houses is the *alacena* or cupboard which is embedded into the wall. Construction is similar to that of the doors of a *trastero*, and the *alacena* doors were usually either puncheon or else had simple eyelet hinges. Because they were often moved from one house to another, with the owners taking only the doors and sometimes the frame, few surviving *alacenas* retain their original shelves.

All furniture in this section is made of pine.

Measurements: Each door — H. 33¼", W. 13"
Date: 19th century, first half
Owner: The Museum of New Mexico
Accession Number: A.72.52-1

These two puncheon doors without their frames illustrate the construction of *alacenas* or built-in wall cupboards and show how the extensions of the outside uprights would fit into a frame embedded in a wall. This eliminated the need for metal hinges, an important factor in New Mexico where there was a scarcity of iron. The plain horizontal and vertical bars of the doors are not common for *alacenas* in New Mexico, and consideration has been given to its possible use as a window before glass arrived. Due to its good condition, however, it probably was used as an *alacena* and not an exterior window. The presence of a carved edging for one shelf, which is photographed under the doors, also points to its use as a cupboard. The pieces now are stained dark brown.

Measurements: Each door — H. 33¼", W. 12"
Date: 19th century, first half
Owner: Private Collection

These two handcarved paneled doors are attached to the frame by hand-wrought eyelets, a type of hinge that uses the minimum of iron. Its original lock is missing, and it now has a hook, a later addition. It is painted dark green and has three shelves. This *alacena* at one time was in the Bouquet Ranch, Pojoaque, New Mexico, an old stage coach stop, now plaqued by the Historic Santa Fe Foundation as being worthy of preservation.

Measurements: Each door — H. 35", W. 16"
Date: 19th century
Owner: Private Collection

The unusual feature of these puncheon doors is the four panel design in each, three of which are carved with varying geometric designs and the fourth left plain. This fairly elaborate carving was possible because of the thickness of the boards (1 5/8 inches thick). This type of carving is usually old, but the open grille above with zigzag uprights seem to be of a later date. Notice the reverse placement of a few of the uprights on the left door. This *alacena* was once painted red.

Measurements: Each door — H. 30½", W. 15¼"
Date: Late 19th century
Owner: Private Collection

Although these puncheon doors have two coats of paint, a relatively recent blue paint over red, there is a sharpness about the carving that does not speak of great age. The top part has zigzags, all carefully placed, while the lower panels are each carved with a six-petaled rosette surrounded by chip carving.

This arrangement combines three of the pieces pictured in this book: a late 18th century table, see page 62, a priest's chair of the first half of the 19th century at the bottom of page 76, and a *repisa* of a similar date on the top of page 59. The *jerga*, or loosely woven wool floor covering, is of that period. The old *santos* and objects add detail to the arrangement as does a geranium which was, and still is, often found on window sills of New Mexican houses.

Repisas

Repisas vary in design and appearance; however, their construction is similar. Sometimes the decorative shelf edgings were done on the bottom instead of the top, where such an edging would have served as a barrier to keep objects from falling off. The makers of these hanging shelves used imagination in embellishing their work, almost always creating a piece with good overall proportions.

All furniture in this section is made of pine.

Measurements: H. 33½", W. 42¼", D. 5½"
Date: 19th century, first half
Owner: Private Collection

This is the only old *repisa* with three shelves that the author has seen. It is mortised and tenoned and has five uprights, the outer two being right next to the end pieces. The horizontals are scalloped above and below, except for the top one where the upper part of the board is lost. The uprights and ends are chip carved. There are two other *repisas* at the Museum of New Mexico, with two shelves instead of three, but of such similar construction and decoration that they must have been made by the same person as this one.

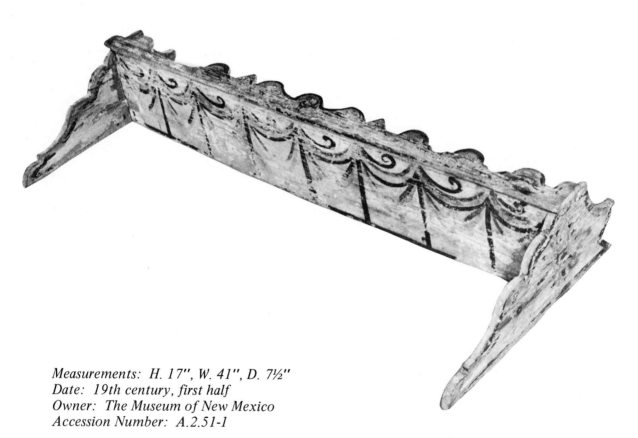

Measurements: H. 17", W. 41", D. 7½"
Date: 19th century, first half
Owner: The Museum of New Mexico
Accession Number: A.2.51-1

This handsome *repisa* is entirely gessoed and painted in *santero* style, with scrolls and floral motifs in black, red, indigo blue and dark brown watercolors. A small bird is painted in the center of the front edge of the shelf, the top of which is carved in a typical Spanish pattern. The end pieces are also cut out on the front in graceful lines, tapering at the bottom.

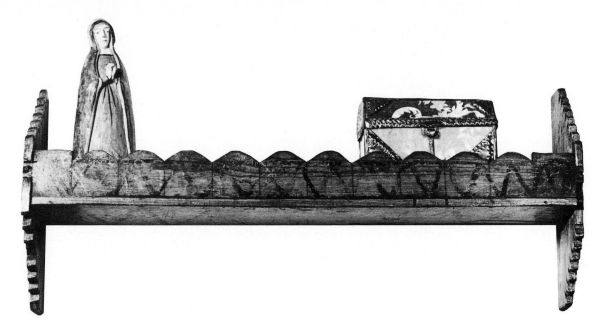

Measurements: *H. 15″, W. 36″, D. 6¼″*
Date: *19th century, first half*
Owner: *Private Collection*

Made of four boards, mortised and tenoned, this *repisa* has some painting left in black "V" designs across the front edge and on the underneath of the shelf. The edge is scalloped on the top, and the ends are cut out in steps both at the top and bottom.

Measurements: *H. 14″, W. 37½″, D. 7½″*
Date: *19th century*
Owner: *Private Collection*

This *repisa* of four heavily adzed and planed boards has grooves on the ends into which the horizontals fit. Square nails are added to strengthen it. This piece gains its character not only from the handsome boards, but also from the variety of cutouts on the edges and on the ends, which also have step ups at the top and a diagonal cutout at the bottom. At least as early as 1923 and until about a decade ago, this *repisa* was in the Juan Rodriguez House, which has been plaqued by the Historic Santa Fe Foundation as being worthy of preservation.

Measurements: H. 21½", W. 41½", D. 5½"
Date: 19th century
Owner: Private Collection

Three uprights carved as splats lend a graceful note to this two-shelf *repisa*. Both edges, which are tenoned into the ends, are scalloped on the bottom, and the lower one is also scalloped on the top. The ends are shaped in a crude scallop design.

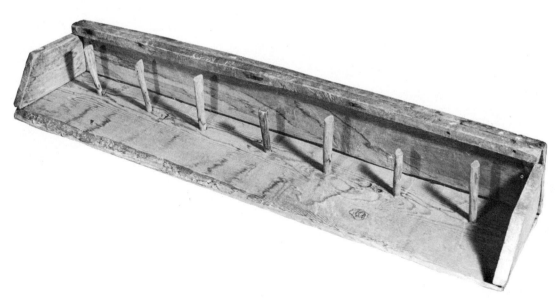

Measurements: H. 10¾", W. 46", D. 6¾"
Date: 19th century, second half
*Owner: Estate of Mrs. Cornelia Gleed Thompson, deceased, on loan to the Museum of
        New Mexico*
Accession Number: L.7.56-35

The special purpose of this *repisa* is indicated by the seven wooden pegs, which were used for hanging coats and other articles that were removed before entering a house. This type was hung on portals and served as 19th century coat closets. Similar *repisas* for the same use sometimes had hooks made of bent over blacksmith nails.

Tables

The earliest New Mexican tables were made for use in churches, as the simple lives of the people did not require such pieces for their own use. Being of moderate size, these formerly ecclesiastical but simple tables are easily used in today's houses. Except for the group of three "serving tables" discussed herein, these pieces are more or less the same in size and height. The author has not located any very large tables of the traditional period, probably because the dining tables as we now know them were not used in New Mexico at that time. Less outside influence is apparent on 19th century tables than is the case with any other category of New Mexican furniture.

All furniture in this section is made of pine.

Measurements: H. 27", diameter of top 32½", frame 21¾"square
Date: 18th century, last quarter
Owner: Private Collection

The six deeply-grooved stretchers, each one of which has cutouts on the bottom, place this table in the 18th century. It was probably used as a side altar table in a mission church or a country church like Las Trampas. The top is made with only two broad boards of different widths and is braced with two cross members. The two cross pieces connected to the top stretchers with nails are later additions in order to hold a drawer which was added subsequently. The stretchers are at three different heights—typical of these tables. At one time this piece was painted red; removal of most, but not all, of this paint has given the table a nice patina.

A close-up of this table top shows an inlayed patch, probably because of a knot hole, contemporary with its construction. This fine workmanship also indicates the 18th century date. The three parallel scratched lines on the table top were to indicate to the maker where he was to put the cross members to brace the top.

A close-up of one side of the same table shows how the maker outlined on the leg where the tenon would go for the stretcher and where to work the bottom of the stretcher for his decorative cutouts.

Measurements: H. 26¼", W. 30½", D. 25½"
Date: 18th century, last quarter
Owner: Private Collection

This rectangular top table is similar to the preceding one, except the medial cross member would indicate that it originally had a drawer. The medial piece is a little lower on the far side, which would keep the drawer from slipping through the table. The top front has a notch that would indicate also the presence of a lock for the drawer.

Measurements: H. 21", W. 29", D. 21¾"
Date: Late 18th century or early 19th century
Owner: Private Collection

The interesting feature of this table is that the six stretchers are not only deeply grooved with cutouts on the lower part, but also have chip carving, creating a triangular pattern. This could be regarded as a transitional piece for the chip carved ones which follow. This table is smaller than the preceding two, but it apparently had a drawer, which would explain the medial piece.

Measurements: H. 25¼", diameter of top 35", frame 20½"square
Date: 1775-1825
Owner: The Historical Society of New Mexico, Museum of New Mexico
Accession Number: A.5.59-10

As a result of the Moorish influence in Spain over many centuries, chip carved furniture was made there. So it is not surprising to find some of the earliest pieces made in New Mexico with this type of decoration. This handsomely proportioned table with a round top has all four skirts chip carved, as well as a small door on a hinge which opens to give access to the whole interior, apparently a substitute by the maker for a drawer. There are three circles on the top incised with a chisel. The hand-carved stretchers with two spools in the center have their ends shaped as dowels. For balance, the ends of the legs have spools too. One brace through two skirts holds the top boards together. Note the iron lock on the left for the door.

Measurements: H. 26¼", W. 36¼", D. 34¼", frame 20½" square
Date: 1775-1825
Owner: Private Collection

This table is of similar construction and design as the previous one except that it has a rectangular top, with a large overhang, a variation in its chip carving and no provision for storage. There is one chisel-incised circle on the top. The stretchers have spools on their full length.

Measurements: H. 22", diameter of top 29½", frame 16½" square
Date: 19th century, first quarter
Owner: Private Collection

This small table has a variation of chip carving on two sides which is repeated on the opposite sides. Three stretchers have three divisions of ring carving, but the fourth is entirely different indicating a replacement. The three spools on the legs are just below the stretchers, instead of being near the floor. The development of this type of table reached most pleasing proportions in this particular piece.

A close-up shows the mortise and tenon of the two skirts as well as the doweled ends of the stretchers. As the result of a sizable piece of wood being broken off the top of the legs a clearer picture is given of the two tenons. Note the addition of nails. The effects of age on the circular top are also apparent.

Measurements: H. 24½", W. 28½", D. 18¾"
Date: 19th century, first quarter
Owner: Private Collection

The same typical chip carved design is on each skirt of this rectangular table, with the addition of chip carving down each leg on both outer sides. These are made by a chisel, first hammered straight on the wood and then with a side stroke of the chisel. The unusual feature of this table is the cutout board on the top, which also has chip carving and which lifts up for access into the entire top for storage. The stretchers are shaped from a square form in the center until they are rounded at the ends for dowels into the legs, typical of many chip carved tables and chairs.

These low tables are called "serving tables" because of their original use. Food was brought in from the kitchen on these pieces, in a tray-like manner, and the table was placed on the floor on which persons sat to eat, there being a dearth of domestic furniture during this period in New Mexico. The few surviving tables of this type are used often now as coffee tables in private houses.

Measurements: H. 14", W. 29½", D. 10½"
Date: 19th century, first half
Owner: Estate of Mrs. Cornelia Gleed Thompson, deceased, on loan to the Museum of
*   New Mexico*
Accession Number: L.7.56-48

This example has grooved stretchers and also skirts, which have decorative cutouts at the bottom. The legs are chamfered at the bottom.

Meaurements: H. 12", W. 31¼", D. 13"
Date: 19th century, first half
Owner: Private Collection

This piece also has cutouts on the skirt. The legs are straighter than those on the previous one, and there are no lower stretchers. This table illustrates a type of repair common to New Mexican furniture before nails became plentiful. When joints were loose, pieces were often strengthened by rawhide, as illustrated here, adding character to the entire piece. The author has seen other tables of this type similarly mended.

Measurements: H. 14", W. 35", D. 12"
Date: 19th century
Owner: Private Collection

This very simple table, with only a grooving on the bottom of the stretcher skirt, seems to have added functional elements in the approximate 1½ inch opening beneath the top. This would have made the table easier to pick up and carry.

Measurements: H. 27", W. 37¼", D. 24¾"
Date: 19th century, first half
Owner: Private Collection

Although this stretcher table has a definite front, it has been used on all sides, as indicated by the wearing of the bottom stretchers on the back and of the slightly lower-placed ones on the sides. The only decoration is on one side, where there are three splat-like uprights set into the two stretchers, the center upright being broader than the outer ones. The top is a single handsome slab of wood, hand adzed and planed, which is doweled to the two cross pieces into which the legs are tenoned, a common construction of New Mexican furniture.

Measurements: H. 25¾", W. 27", D. 17¼"
Date: 19th century, first half
Owner: Private Collection

The main feature of this small table are the hand-carved spindles, three on the front and back and two on each end. These are complemented by the carving of spools and rings on the lower part of the legs. The drawer, which could be an old addition, is dovetailed.

Measurements: H. 25¾", W. 26", D. 18½"
Date: 19th century, first half
Owner: The School of American Research, on loan to
*   the Museum of New Mexico*
Accession Number: A.7.49-4

This table, which at first appears similar to the preceding one, also has hand-carved spindles, three at front and back and two at the ends. However, as it has no drawer and the legs are carved in spools and rings between the stretchers as well as below the bottom stretchers, the table has an entirely different character. Notice the incised lines on the stretchers above and below the spindles to indicate to the maker where he should make holes for the spindles so that they would be evenly spaced.

Measurements: H. 18½", diameter of top 26¼", frame 19½" by 16"
Date: Circa 1850
Owner: The Spanish Colonial Arts Society, Inc., on loan to the Museum of New Mexico
Accession Number: L.5.56-20

The previous owner called this a "chocolate table", and it certainly could have been used for that purpose, as it was a custom among the Spanish to serve chocolate in the afternoons, a tradition which is still being followed. The boards of this table are hand adzed and planed, and the stretchers are mortised and tenoned. The only decoration is on the front stretcher where "S" curves are carved on the bottom. Notice on this table also the maker's incised marks to indicate the placement of the carving. There is little overhang of the top, and the proportions of this low table are pleasing.

Measurements: H. 26½", W. 26", D. 10½"
Date: 19th century
Owner: The American Museum in Britain, Bath, England
Accession Number: 60.608
Photographer: Derek Balmer

This plain table is typical of those made for small chapels and *moradas* during the 19th century. The drawer, which probably had a rawhide thong as a pull, would be used for storing articles used in services. The top is one slab thicker at one end than the other. Note the cross pieces under the top and how they fit into the legs.

Measurements: H. 21¾", W. 26½", D. 19¼"
Date: 19th century, second half
Owner: Private Collection

This nicely proportioned table is reminiscent of 17th century Spanish tables, except for the chamfered legs and knobbed feet. This shows the conservative element and traditionally oriented nature of the Spanish people. The top of the table is one slab of thick wood (about 1½ inches thick). All four skirts have a carving of "S" curves starting from the center. The four lower stretchers are at almost the same level; this would not have been the case if the piece had been made earlier, as it was easier to tenon stretchers at different levels on the legs.

Measurements: H. 20¾", W. 19¾", D. 17¾"
Date: 19th century, last quarter
Owner: Private Collection

This useful table shows outside influence, but it is unmistakably New Mexican in character. The frame is of mortise and tenon construction in the traditional manner. There is no
overhang of the top, which is one piece of wood. The drawer is dovetailed, and the ring
pull is a later addition. The legs are shaped in spools and rings.

Chairs

As was the case with tables, the earliest chairs were made for churches and, occasionally, for houses where priests and other dignitaries frequently visited. The first domestic chairs were simple ones with only chip carving decorating the straight lines of those pieces. Subsequently, a considerable variety of designs and shapes developed during the 19th century, although traditional construction elements continued to be used. It is interesting that in almost all cases until about 1900, these side chairs were small in size.

All furniture in this section is made of pine unless otherwise noted.

Measurements: H. 38¾", at seat 19¼", W. 25¼", D. 24"
Date: 18th century, last quarter
Owner: The Museum of New Mexico
Accession Number: A.62.23-1

This impressive piece is one of the largest chairs made in colonial New Mexico. It is called a "priest's chair" and came from a church in northern New Mexico. Two similar ones, but with their arms sawed off, are in the Museum of New Mexico and probably came from the same church. Notice the decorative elements of this chair: deeply grooved rails and front stretcher with "M" cutouts; shaped splats, which vary in design at the two levels. The stiles slant back above the seat in typical New Mexican style. The arms have a slight curve ending in a hook shape. Mortise and tenon construction is clearly visible, and the boards are hand adzed and planed.

Measurements: H. 38¾", at seat 17", W. 21½", D. 16¾"
Date: 19th century, first half
Owner: Private Collection

Although somewhat more crudely made than the preceding one, this priest's chair has dignity and a handsome patina created by age and by the wearing off of old paint. One's eye is drawn to the cutouts and grooving where the two top rail boards meet and on the seat rail. Again, the stiles slant back above the seat, and they end in a finial of four carved step ups, a common detail in New Mexican furniture. Notice how deeply the front stretcher is worn.

Measurements:
  Chair on left: H. 32", at seat 18", W. 18", D. 16½"
  Chair on right: H. 31½", at seat 15¼", W. 18", D. 18"
Date: Late 18th century to about 1830
Owner: Private Collection

Many of these chip carved side chairs were made around the turn of the 19th century. Each piece varies; however, they are similar in design and with respect to the areas on which there is carving—the rails and sometimes the stiles. These two typical examples were photographed together not only because of their similar style, but also to illustrate a mistake which was not uncommon in chip carved furniture here. In the chair on the right the back rails are put on upside down; compare the carving with that on the seat rail. No doubt the maker chip carved the board first, then cut the tenon incorrectly, so that in order to use the board at all it had to be inserted into the mortise of each stile in the reverse manner shown. The author has also seen this mistake in several chip carved tables.

Measurements: H. 32¾", at seat 17¼", W. 16½", D. 14"
Date: Late 18th century to 1830
Owner: Private Collection

A characteristic of the seats of these chip carved chairs is a simple flare creating an overhang on the front corners. This chair is in almost perfect condition except for the loss of a flare on one corner of the seat, perhaps done when someone was using the chair as a sawhorse to saw wood. Because of the overhang, these seats were vulnerable to general wear as well as abuse, and few chairs have their original seats. On this chair all the chip carved rails are attached correctly. The seat is pegged to the rails. Notice how the rungs are doweled through the legs, and wedges have been inserted into the center of the dowels for added strength.

A close-up of the back shows how chip carving was done with one or two strokes of a chisel, creating an often-repeated pattern plus variations.

These two chairs present a feeling and appearance entirely different from other New Mexican chairs. These were made of whittled hardwood, probably local scrub oak, instead of pine, and their seats were made of laced rawhide thongs. No doubt these chairs were fairly common early in the 19th century in mountain villages, where small hardwood poles were available and rawhide was plentiful. Shepherds made beds of similar construction using poles and rawhide, which they made and left at each camp site.

Measurements: H. 30", at seat 14", W. at back 14", W. at front 12¼", D. 12½"
Date: 19th century, first quarter
Owner: Private Collection

The slats are shaped to a point in the center and are attached to the stiles by wooden pegs. The stiles slant slightly back from the seat, and note how the seat narrows toward the front. The left seat rung protrudes through the leg. Notice also how the front legs are splayed.

Meaurements: H. 32¼", at seat 16", W. 16½", D. 16½"
Date: 19th century, first quarter
Owner: The Spanish Colonial Arts Society, Inc., on loan to the Museum of New Mexico
Accession Number: L.5.56-34

Two slats on the back are missing, and two of the rungs are replacements. This chair also retains its wooden pegs, and the rungs are doweled. Note the old rawhide repair on the right front leg; compare this to the repairs on the table at the top of page 69.

Measurements: H. 31½", at seat 16", W. 15¼", D. 16½"
Date: 19th century, second quarter
Owner: Estate of Mrs. Cornelia Gleed Thompson,
*   deceased, on loan to the Museum of New Mexico*
Accession Number: L.7.56-11

Many chairs of this type were made in New Mexico beginning in the second quarter of the 19th century. They are best described as New Mexican adaptations of the Directory and Empire styles. The general features are curved lines. This chair illustrates these features in its stiles and legs. Even the two slats are carved to curve in a horizontal direction. Construction is, however, still the traditional New Mexican style of through mortise and tenon.

Measurements: H. 33", at seat 17½", W. 16½", D. 17"
Date: 1840's
Owner: Private Collection

This particular chair can be said to have more of an Empire style influence in that the stiles are only slightly concave, and there is no curve at the top. The slats are flat boards, not curved horizontally, but shaped on the top and bottom. These New Mexican chairs are also sometimes referred to as being in the style of Duncan Phyfe, a celebrated New York furniture maker in the first quarter of the 19th century.

Measurements: H. 27″, at seat 12″, W. 14″, D. 14½″
Date: 19th century, second quarter
Owner: Private Collection

No one could imagine that this small chair of unusual proportions was made anywhere but New Mexico. The wood is thick for the size of the piece, and the seat is unusually low, undoubtedly made for a small person or a child. The rear legs repeat in reverse the strong curve of the front legs. The heavy top rail is rounded at the top to fit into the curve of the stiles. The front rung, which protrudes through the legs, is a replacement.

Measurements: H. 31″, at seat 16″, W. 15¼″, D. 18″
Date: Circa 1850
Owner: Private Collection

Similar in type to the three preceding chairs, this simple, straightforward piece exhibits more outside influences than others. Notice the straight front legs, which do not taper in the usual New Mexican way. This chair is reminiscent of the Sheraton style; however, the broad splat is shaped in a typical Spanish New Mexican manner.

Measurements: H. 33½″, at seat 18″, W. 19¾″, D. 20″
Date: Circa 1850
Owner: Private Collection

This priest's, or arm, chair has typical New Mexican features: mortise and tenon construction, backward slant of the stiles above the seat, narrowing of front legs from the seat to the floor, the front and back stretchers at different heights. Again notice how the front stretcher is worn from use. There is an almost identical chair in the Museum of New Mexico, which once belonged to Padre Jose Antonio Martinez of Taos, who was an influential and controversial personage in New Mexico during the middle of the 19th century. His chair was acquired in 1916 by the Historical Society of New Mexico from the Martinez-Montaner family.

Measurements: H. 34″, at seat 16½″, W. 16½″, D. 15″
Date: 19th century, second half
Owner: Private Collection

The honesty and simplicity of this chair give it a strong character. An artist once called it a beautiful piece of sculpture. It is of typical New Mexican construction and has a slanting back, deep skirts and tapering legs.

Measurements: H. 23½", at seat 13¼", W. 13½", D. 14½"
Date: 19th century, third quarter
Owner: Private Collection

This is one of the rare instances in New Mexican furniture when the name of the maker is known. Through family records of the descendants, who are the present owners of this chair, its maker is known to be Jose Manuel Gonzales, who lived in Agua Fria; he died in 1880 and is buried outside the village church there. This small chair is well worn and has had many layers of paint, the latest being black. The two boards, which form the top rail, are carved where they meet to form a bow design. The rails are molded with a plane, the stiles slant back and the seat is cut out to accomodate the tops of the front legs. All three stretchers are worn, particularly the one in front.

Measurements: H. 15", at seat 8", W. 10", D. 9¾"
Date: 19th century, second half
Owner: Private Collection

This straight little chair was obviously made for a child. It has "FINA" carved on the bottom of the back stretcher; this is the diminutive form of many Spanish names. The hand planed seat is doweled to the two boards above the legs. The front legs are tenoned into those boards, which in turn are tenoned into the stiles, an unusual construction. The entire chair is well worn.

84

Current exhibits at the Museum of Albuquerque include this room. Details of a checkered *jerga* (loosely woven wool floor covering), tin sconces and a typical corner fireplace provide an appropriate setting for a little chip carved chair with spindles, a *taramita* and a child's bed with a colcha embroidered bedspread—all of which were furniture used in 19th century New Mexico.

Benches and Stools

Benches, also, were first made for use in churches for the seating of dignitaries. Note the similarity in feeling and design of the first bench pictured to that of the priest's chair at the beginning of the previous category. Later, individual families made and owned benches for use as their private pews. As each varied in size and design, the overall grouping in a church must have been a picturesque sight. Such a scene was recreated several years ago when the Museum of New Mexico had an exhibit of a 19th century chapel. Many of these benches have survived. On the other hand, there are few little stools, or *taramitas*, presently known to exist. Perhaps, as they were so constantly used in the average household, hard wear finally resulted in most of them being destroyed.

All furniture in this section is made of pine.

Measurements: H. 33", at seat 19½", W. 33", D. 19½"
Date: Circa 1800
Owner: The Historical Society of New Mexico, Museum of New Mexico
Accession Number: A.5.59-26
Photographer: Laura Gilpin

Of exceptionally good proportions, this early hand adzed and planed bench is in a typical colonial New Mexican style. The overall effect is that of a "geometric" piece, with "M" and triangular cutouts on the rails, emphasized by deep grooving on the rails and front stretcher. There are five splats of a similar diamond-shaped design on both the back and below the seat. Compare this for design and feeling with the chair at the top of page 76. The use of multiple splats seems to appear only in furniture of New Mexico, Spain and its other colonies.

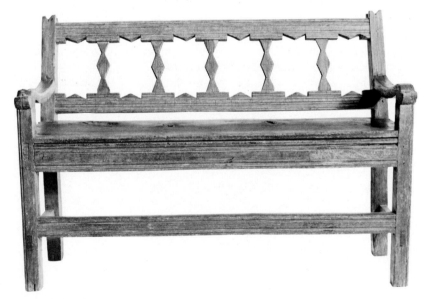

Measurements: H. 35½", at seat 20", W. 51", D. 17¼"
Date: Early 19th century
Owner: Private Collection

Although similar in some ways to the preceding one, this bench is somewhat simpler in design, particularly below the seat, and is much longer. The top of each stile is cut out in the center leaving points on the four corners, creating a quadrifid finial. The arms slope at the center ending in a rounded form. No adzing is evident on this piece, but it is hand planed. It was once painted robin's egg blue.

Measurements: H. 33½", at seat 16½", W. 64½", D. 19½"
Date: 1820-30
Owner: The Museum of New Mexico
Accession Number: A.72.19-1

This even longer bench is a handsome and elaborate example made of hand adzed and planed boards. The most unusual part is the construction and design on the back. The three uprights, each of one piece of wood, are fitted flush to the back of the central rail, and the uprights are tenoned into the rails above and below. Designs on the central rail match and complement those on the other two back rails. The cutouts on the bottom of the seat rail provide a pleasing lower border for the multiple designs above the seat level. Deep grooving of the rails and stretchers and the termination of each stile in a carved ball add other elements of finish to this piece.

Measurements: H. 42½", at seat 19", W. 72", D. 18"
Date: 19th century
Owner: The Historical Society of New Mexico, Museum of New Mexico
Accession Number: B 83/68 MNM
Photographer: Laura Gilpin

This somewhat cruder large bench without arms is of an entirely different nature from the preceding ones. Emphasis is on the compass incising on the single back rail, with its top and bottom carved in "M" and "S" designs, as is the top of the seat rail, and the unusual hour-glass carving on the stiles ending in pyramid step-up finials.

Measurements: H. 6¼", W. 11¾", D. 6"
Date: 18th century, last quarter
Owner: Private Collection

Made of five pieces of wood this *taramita* or stool has no carving or decoration except that the leg boards have a rounded arch. There is an overhang of the seat and side pieces at the ends. The legs fit into the seat, which is doweled, with nails being a later addition. The slits at each side of the seat are a continuance of the cuts to accomodate the legs. The stool was once painted blue, and its appearance now is one of a sturdy seat of heavy, aged boards.

Measurements: H. 7½", W. 16¼", D. 7¼"
Date: 19th century
Owner: The Spanish Colonial Arts Society, Inc., on loan to the Museum of Albuquerque
Accession Number: L.5.60-30

This *taramita* is also made of five pieces of wood, but the fifth one seems to have been added at one end for strengthening, and the fourth one is original along the side for the same purpose. The leg boards also have a round arch at the foot. The seat board has the edges slightly planed, which makes it look thinner than it is.

Measurements: H. 11¾", W. 24", D. 9¼"
Date: 19th century
Owner: Private Collection

The decoration of this well proportioned *taramita* consists of grooving at the bottom of the skirts and a Gothic arch at the foot of each leg board. Each leg is mortised and tenoned in two places to the seat. The skirts are flush with the legs. This and the two preceding stools were the usual seats in old New Mexican homes, in addition to the "built-in" adobe *bancos* along the walls.

Other Furniture

This category includes miscellaneous types of furniture which were made in the last half of the 19th century and show considerable outside influences. Beds were not common in New Mexico until new residents arrived from the east who were used to such conveniences; most New Mexicans still slept on mattresses on the floor and continued to do so, in rural areas, until well into the 20th century. The cradle is a pleasing piece and the only one which the author has found that he regards as New Mexican made. Undoubtedly, Victorian styles influenced the cutout galleries of the washstands pictured. The author hopes at some future time to be able to locate desks made in New Mexico earlier. Although mentioned in wills in the early 19th century, either none of these has survived or else they had been imported into New Mexico, which is unlikely for that period. The chair table pictured is an interesting New Mexican adaptation of a specialty piece made in this manner on the East Coast at least 100 years earlier.

All furniture in this section is made of pine.

Measurements: H. 30", at seat 14¾", W. 81½", D. 30"
Date: 19th century, second half
Owner: Private Collection

This deep daybed with its French influence has attractive "S"-curved stiles and an outward flare of the legs. Compare this with the chairs on pages 80 and 81. Construction is through mortise and tenon on the central rail and on the seat rails, each of which have double mortise and tenons into the legs, a feature uncommon to New Mexico. The top eight-sided rail and five handcarved spindles at each end are doweled into sockets of the stiles and rails, respectively, and turn freely. Old blue paint adds to the attractiveness of this daybed.

Measurements: H. 24½", at seat 15½", W. 78", D. 22¼"
Date: 19th century, second half
Owner: Private Collection

There seems to be less outside influence in the style of this simpler daybed with its more typical narrow depth. The stiles, made of thick boards, curve outward only slightly, and the legs taper. Double mortise and tenon construction again appears on all the seat rails. This was possibly to strengthen the construction, due to the long front and back seat rails. At each end there are seven handcarved spindles firmly doweled to the two lathed end rails. These rails are doweled in a peculiar manner to the stiles: half of the dowels go through, while the others do not, which indicates that the maker was not a professional. This daybed is painted earth red.

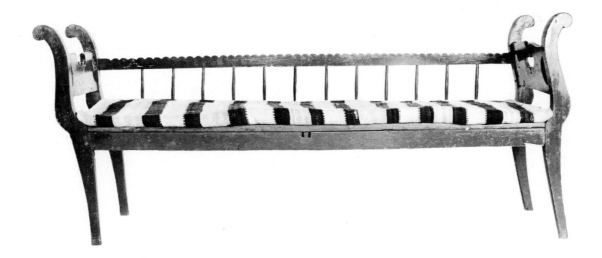

Measurements: H. 32", at seat 17", W. 76", D. 20¼"
Date: 19th century, second half
Owner: Private Collection

Although showing much outside influence both in the extreme flare of the top of the stiles and in the absence of through mortise and tenon construction, this daybed with a back, or a settee, still shows strong New Mexican influences in its tapering legs, the left front one being a replacement, and the unusual and not matching cutout designs on the top of the broad end rails. The narrow scalloped back rail and thin spindles add a delicacy to the piece.

Measurements: H. 26½", W. 31¼", D. 25"
Date: 19th century, second half
Owner: Private Collection

This cradle of pleasing design came from Las Trampas in the early 1930's. An open feeling is created by the spindles. Notice how the two outer ones at each end slant; these balance the similar slope of the legs and stiles, which end in step-up finials. A half rosette surrounded by two scallops is carved on the inside at each end. Holes on the lower rails now hold rope, but probably rawhide was originally used.

Measurements: H. 30½", W. 20½", D. 19½"
Date: 19th century, last half
Owner: Private Collection

This simple washstand with a drawer and constructed with nails has a gallery on three sides, all of which have cutouts. The legs between the skirt and bottom shelf are chamfered. Although there is a strong outside influence in this piece, the construction is through mortise and tenon.

Measurements: H. 27½", W. 23¼", D. 18¼"
Date: 19th century, last half
Owner: Private Collection

This washstand, which is painted green, shows less outside influence. The handmade appliqued ribbed wood on the front and sides is of interest, as the author has seen at least two *trasteros* much-decorated with these applied ribbed pieces, and they are supposed to have come from the area of Taos or Mora. This washstand has a gallery with flamboyant cutouts, and the sides are also ribbed. The legs are chamfered between the skirt and bottom shelf and also below the shelf. The drawer has appliqued pieces in the shape of leaves on either side of the pull.

Measurements: H. 53", W. 24½", D. 26"
Date: 19th century, last quarter
Owner: Private Collection

This desk, made near the end of the 19th century, has a top which lifts, a replacement, and sliding doors, an unusual feature in any New Mexican furniture. The two doors are each made of two boards decorated with hand grooved moldings, with the one down the center covering the joining of the boards. Front and side panels are also molded. Although desks were mentioned in wills as early as one in 1814, none seems to have survived. No doubt in earlier periods desks were brought from Mexico by dignitaries, but taken back with them when they left New Mexico. The present owners found this desk in Llano near Dixon with a chicken nesting in it. This was in 1965 when the 75-year old Spanish American man who sold it to them said he had used it as a child and his father had made it.

Measurements:
    As table: H. 32½", Top 54¼" by 34½"
    As chair: H. 56½", at seat 20¼", W. 27¾", D. 21¼"
Date: 19th century, last half
Owner: Private Collection

Of the three chair tables the author has seen, all made of sawmill lumber, this one has the strongest New Mexican feeling with its mortise and tenon construction, paneled front and ends with moldings hand grooved on all four sides and legs broadening at seat level. The top is of five boards, which are nailed to the two cross members, each of which has a hole through which a dowel is placed to go through the hole in each back stile. (This is visible when the piece is open as a chair.) Thus the top swings on a pair of dowels and also can be removed at any time, making the piece easier to move. The ends still have most of their original carved open designs, but three of the half circles near the center of the design have been lost. The top of the table has a compass outlined six-pointed star design. The entire chair table is painted a nice earth red.

Photographer: Derek Balmer

With the help of cooperative British craftsmen, the author, in 1961, installed this room, which is on permanent exhibition, in the American Museum in Britain at Bath, England. The daybed and carved chest sit on a checkered jerga (loosely woven wool floor covering). A typical *trastero* and a chip carved chair are seen on the right. A corner fireplace surrounded by *santos* and domestic implements and a geranium potted in a tin can on the window sill complete this interpretation of an all-purpose 19th century room.

Glossary

Adz: a tool having a thin arching blade set at right angles to the handle and thus different from an ax; it is used to trim the surface of wood. See photograph on page 17.

Alacena: a regional Spanish term for a cupboard built into the wall.

Appliqued: applied or laid on ornamentation; herein used interchangeably with "applied."

Auger: a tool for boring holes in wood.

Awl: a pointed instrument for piercing small holes. See photograph on page 17.

Banco: Spanish for a bench; often used in New Mexico to mean seating ledges built out from the walls of a room.

Beaded: a semicircular concave edge made with a beading plane.

Beveled: cutout at a shape so that surfaces are not at right angles, creating a slant or inclination of such surfaces.

Chamfered: the cutting off of corners or edges, such as legs of furniture.

Chip carved: hand-carving done with strokes of a chisel.

Crest: the uppermost horizontal element on a *trastero*, both front and sides.

Dovetail: two pieces of wood cut in such a way that one with tongues (shaped like the tail of a dove) fits tightly into cutouts of the second piece to make a strong joint.

Dowel: a wooden pin which secures two pieces of wood together.

Escutcheon: a metal shield to protect wood, or for an ornament, around a key hole.

Eyelet hinge: a metal ring, the ends of which can be bent outward and over to fasten it in place.

Finial: ornamentation that forms the upper extremity of a pinnacle, as on the stile of a chair.

Gallery: a barrier or railing along the edge of a table, shelf, etc.

Gesso: a gypsum compound applied to wood as a ground for painting.

Grooved: cut so as to form channels or grooves.

Hasp: a hinged clasp or fastening for a lid which snaps into a lock, as on a chest.

Lathed: cut by a tool which holds and rotates the piece while it is formed and shaped by a cutting tool.

Mortise and tenon: joining boards by cutting a rectangular hole, a mortise, into which a tongue, the tenon, is inserted. See text for special New Mexican characteristics.

Mudejar: styles resulting from Moorish modifications of Spanish designs.

Plane: a tool for smoothing wood and forming moldings. See photograph on page 17.

Post: a piece of wood fixed firmly in an upright position, especially as a stay or support.

Puncheon door: a door so constructed with a piece of wood extending above and below the door so it can swing into sockets of the frame, eliminating the need for metal hinges. In architecture this puncheon construction is sometimes called a pintle hinge.

Rail: a horizontal connecting member between two supports.

Repisa: Spanish for a bracket or hanging shelf.

Rung: one of the round horizontal supports of a chair.

Santero: a regional Spanish term for a person making *santos*, or holy images.

Skirt: that horizontal part which serves as a rim, border, etc.

Slat: a horizontal board between the stiles above the seat rail.

Spindle: a short decorative upright piece, turned or hand-carved.

Splat: a flat member of a chair back rising from the seat rail or one just above it to the top rail.

Splayed: slanting, spread out, having an oblique angle so as to flare.

Stile: one of the upright pieces or primary members of a frame into which the secondary members are secured.

Stretcher: the bracing member reaching between and steadying the legs of chairs, tables, etc.

Taramita: diminutive for the Spanish word *tarima*, meaning a low bench or stool; hence, a little stool.

Tenon: a projecting member left by cutting away the wood around it for insertion into a mortise to make a joint. See text for special New Mexican characteristics.

Tongue and groove: a projecting rib on one edge of a board together with a corresponding groove into which this rib fits on the edge of another board.

Trastero: New Mexican Spanish for a free standing cupboard.